# The Global Marketplace

# Making the Trade

## Stocks, Bonds, and Other Investments

**Aaron Healey**

Heinemann Library
Chicago, Illinois

**www.heinemannraintree.com**
Visit our website to find out
more information about
Heinemann-Raintree books.

**To order:**
☎ Phone 888-454-2279
🖳 Visit www.heinemannraintree.com
to browse our catalog and order online.

Edited by Adam Miller and Andrew Farrow
Designed by Ryan Frieson
Original illustrations © Capstone Global Library,
  Ltd., 2011
Illustrated by Planman Technologies (India) Pvt.,
  Ltd.
Maps by Mapping Specialists, Ltd.
Picture research by Hannah Taylor
Originated by Capstone Global Library, Ltd.
Printed and bound in China by South China
  Printing Company, Ltd.

15 14 13 12 11 10
10 9 8 7 6 5 4 3 2 1

**Library of Congress Cataloging-in-Publication
Data**
Healey, Aaron.
  Making the trade : stocks, bonds, and other
investments / Aaron Healey.
      p. cm.—(The global marketplace)
  Includes bibliographical references and index.
  ISBN 978-1-4329-3931-1 (hc)
  1. Investments. 2. Saving and investment. 3.
Portfolio management.  I. Title.
  HG4521.H45 2011
  332.6—dc22                    2010004094

**Acknowledgments**

The author and publisher are grateful to the
following for permission to reproduce copyright
material: Alamy Images p. **34** (© les polders); Corbis
pp. **35** (Craig Pulsifer), **43** (Eleanor Bentall), **44**
(epa/Justin Lane), **47** (Reuters/Larry Downing), **48**
(Minnesota Historical Society); Corbis SABA
p. **27** (Greg Smith); Getty Images pp. **25**
(Bloomberg/Daniel Acker), **30** (Jim Bourg);
Photolibrary pp. **4** (age fotostock/Casey Kelbaugh),
**6** (Radius Images), **8** (Rafael Macia), **12, 14**
(Jean-Pierre Boutet), **18** (Creatas), **41** (Blend
Images/Andersen Ross); Rex Features p. **10**
(Edward Webb).

Cover photograph of the trading floor of the New
York Stock Exchange,  March 2008, reproduced with
permission of Getty Images (Scott Wintrow).

We would like to thank Michael Miller and
Laura J. Hensley for their invaluable help in the
preparation of this book.

# Contents

Some words are printed in bold, **like this**. You can find out what they mean by looking in the glossary.

# A World of Investment

If you use your time to read this book, what is in it for you? You hope that by putting your time into reading it, you will gain useful knowledge in return. Your decision to read this book is an **investment** of your time.

As with any investment, you are taking a **risk**. You are betting and hoping that reading this book will be time well spent. If you do not learn anything, you will know that you have made a bad bet. The time you spent will be lost, and the chance to do other things with your time—such as watching a movie or hanging out with friends—will be gone as well.

## Risks and rewards

Just as you take a risk when you decide where to **invest** your time, people take risks when they decide to invest their money. The world is full of opportunities for investing money. Each carries its own risks and rewards.

Some kinds of investments carry less risk, such as putting money into a **savings** account. The chances of losing the money are very small, but you will also make less money. Other kinds of investments are riskier, such as putting money into a new business. You will lose your money if the business does not succeed. But if the business becomes a multimillion-dollar success, then you stand to make a lot of money.

With every investment decision comes a hidden cost. This is the cost of not being able to invest the money in another way or to spend it on something else, because you already used your money for the investment. This cost is known as the opportunity cost.

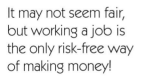

It may not seem fair, but working a job is the only risk-free way of making money!

## Easy money?

If you have worked at a job, then you may have already wished that there could be an easier way to make money. Making money is usually not easy. It takes hard work and lots of time. But investing offers the promise of making money quickly, with little effort. That is why people look for ways to invest their money to make more money. Of course, if people make unwise investments, all their hard-earned money can be lost.

## Investment choices

As technology spreads and the world becomes more interconnected, the opportunities for investing money increase. In this book, you will learn about the ways people are investing their money around the world today, and the risks and rewards available at every turn.

It might seem as though you will never save enough money to invest. But someday, with luck and hard work, you will be able to make choices about where to invest your money. This chart shows some of the many investment options available to people around the world, as well as where you can read more about them in this book.

| DIFFERENT KINDS OF INVESTMENTS | |
|---|---|
| **Form of investment** | **What it does** |
| Checking account (page 14) | Keeps money conveniently available, but it may not earn any money |
| Savings account (page 15) | Money can be withdrawn when you need it, but it earns money slowly |
| Money market account (page 16) | Makes more than a savings account, but money is less available for use |
| Certificate of deposit (CD) (page 16) | Makes a set amount of money over time, but only if money is not taken out |
| Bond (page 18) | Earns a moderate amount of money, with a small risk of losing money |
| Stock (page 24) | Can earn or lose a lot of money |
| Real estate (houses and apartments) (page 32) | Usually rises in value over a long period of time, but values can fall, too. There are costs and fees to buying, and it is not always easy to resell. |
| Commodities such as gold, oil, or wheat (page 35) | Value can rise or fall due to world events that affect supply and demand |

# The Market for Money

As the chart on page 5 shows, there are many different kinds of investments. They are all part of the world financial **markets**.

A market is a system that allows people to trade one thing for another. There are many kinds of markets, for everything from cotton to houses. Items such as cotton and houses are "**goods**," or items of **value**, that can be bought and sold. The **price** (amount charged) is determined by what buyers are willing to pay for it, and what sellers are willing to sell it for.

## Where are markets located?

People tend to think of markets as having one physical location. This is often the case, as when we go to a shoe store where buyers and sellers interact, or to a bank where borrowers and savers go to do business.

But markets do not have to be located in any particular place. For example, people have bought goods from catalogs for years without leaving home. Buying and selling from home is becoming even more common today thanks to the Internet. Whether you live in the United States, United Kingdom, Argentina, South Africa, or South Korea, you can buy and sell almost anything on auction websites such as eBay.

Markets exist anywhere and anytime people interact with each other by buying and selling goods or **services** (acts performed for a fee) at mutually agreeable prices.

Malls are a kind of market.

# The language of money

Terms such as *money*, **income**, *wealth*, and *net worth* are often used when discussing finances. What does each of these terms mean, and how are they different?

## Money

Money is how people pay for the things they want, and it includes cash, checks, and debit cards. It is a way to create exchanges or to make payments. In the United States, money is counted in dollars. The United Kingdom has the pound, Japan has the yen, and Euros are used in many European countries.

Money is also a method for measuring the market value of goods and services. For example, the amounts that people charge for services such as babysitting, walking a neighbor's dog, or running a fruit or lemonade stand show what the current value is of that service.

## Income

Income is how much money you earn from your job (sometimes called a salary), or from gifts and allowances. It can also be the money you make from investments.

## Wealth and net worth

The terms *wealth* and *net worth* are often used to mean the same thing. Net worth is the market value (potential selling price) of your **assets** (items of value) minus your **debts** (money owed) on a given date. If your only asset is a computer worth $2,000, but you owe a debt to someone of $1,500, then your net worth is positive—$500. If your debt is greater than the worth of your assets, then you have a negative net worth. Of course, you should always try to make sure that your net worth is positive!

## Financial markets

Financial markets are like other markets—but in these markets, money is what is "bought" and "sold." Financial markets are all around us. People can invest money from almost anywhere in the world by making a deposit in a savings account electronically (see pages 14 and 15), or buying **stocks** and **bonds** over the Internet (see pages 18 to 31). Or people can borrow money from almost anywhere by using a **credit** card to make a purchase.

## Joining the financial markets

You may not realize it, but when you put money in the bank or make another investment, you become part of the financial markets.

For example, when you put money in a savings account, you are temporarily "selling" your money to the bank. You might look for a bank that will pay you the most **interest**, which is the additional money you get for agreeing to place your savings with the bank.

Banks, in turn, lend out your money to people around the world, using **loans** (money given with repayment conditions), credit cards, and other means. But they do not simply give people all the money they ask for. In addition to the money they give, they charge interest. This extra money helps keep banks in business.

If nobody invested their money, businesses would not have money available for major projects like the Burj Khalifa, the world's tallest building.

## Fueling the global marketplace

If banks did not take in savings, they would not be able to offer loans to people, including businesses. And if people did not invest in other kinds of financial tools like stocks and bonds, this would further prevent businesses from getting money.

What would happen if no one invested their money? Businesses around the world would eventually stop working. They would not have the money to develop and introduce new products, build new buildings, buy necessary equipment, or hire new workers. Because of this lack of money, businesses would need to lay off workers.

In addition to losing their jobs, people would suffer in other ways if everyone stopped investing. Banks would not be able to offer loans, and without loans many families would not be able to buy new cars and houses, make home improvements, or send their children to college.

In these ways, the money that people invest is the fuel that keeps the global marketplace running. Without investment and healthy financial markets, world **economies** would collapse (see box below).

### The credit crunch

In 2008 and 2009, the world got a taste of what life would be like if financial markets were not working. During this period, banks suddenly stopped lending much money. It happened because banks around the world had offered loans to too many people who could not repay them. These loans had been traded to other banks around the world until nobody was sure just who had these "bad" loans.

Because of the loans, banks began to run out of money. Even when banks had money to lend, because of their recent bad experiences, many banks became afraid of lending money. Many people began taking their money out of banks and other investments. This lack of available money became known as "the credit crunch."

The entire economy of the United States, and even the world economy, seemed to be in danger of collapse. People worried that once businesses became unable to borrow money, they would quickly fail. To prevent disaster, leaders in the United States voted to loan $700 billion to banks to ensure they had enough money to lend. The immediate situation improved, but lending remained slow for more than a year.

## Bringing people together

As you've just learned, investing keeps the economy moving. People who have money to invest look for ways to make the most of their money. Meanwhile, businesses are eager to receive these investments to help them grow. To achieve these goals, **investors** (people who invest money) and businesses meet in the financial markets.

Financial markets coordinate the amount that savers want to save with the amount that people such as businesses want to borrow. They do much the same thing for savings that other markets do for shoes, jewelry, toothpaste, and other products.

## Supply and demand

Consider the market for a common product, such as shoes. Every day individuals called **consumers** in countries throughout the world plan on buying a pair of shoes in their size. They create a **demand** for shoes. Meanwhile, a smaller (but still large) number of individuals called **producers** throughout the world are making plans to produce and distribute shoes. They are creating the **supply** of shoes.

Have you ever had a hard time finding a certain pair of sneakers? If so, the demand for that style was greater than the supply.

Producers cannot possibly check with everyone interested in buying shoes to find out what they want to buy. Yet if the number of shoes consumers plan on buying is greater than the number producers plan on selling, there will be a shortage of shoes. As a result, some buyers will not find the shoes they want. And if the number of shoes consumers plan on buying is fewer than the number producers plan on selling, producers will have a surplus of shoes, meaning they will have too many left over.

## Finding an equilibrium point

Fortunately, the market helps to solve problems like this. It does so by affecting prices. The price is set by supply and demand.

When consumers want more shoes than producers are willing to supply at the current price, the market price of shoes will increase. The supply is not meeting the demand, and so consumers have to pay more if they really want the shoes. Similarly, when more producers want to sell shoes at the current price, but there is not enough demand to buy them all, then the market price of shoes will decrease. Producers will have to be willing to charge less money if they want to sell all of their shoes.

The market price will reach the point at which consumers' plans to buy shoes and producers' plans to sell shoes meet at the same point, known as the equilibrium point (see chart below).

The same type of price changes bring together buyers and sellers in markets for thousands of different products. Buyers decide how many shoes, toothbrushes, CDs, DVDs, books, or meals they want at the current prices. This interaction between consumers and producers is known as the law of supply and demand. It is the markets at work.

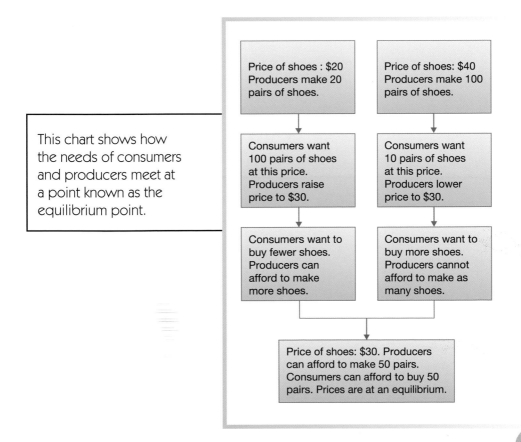

This chart shows how the needs of consumers and producers meet at a point known as the equilibrium point.

Price of shoes : $20
Producers make 20 pairs of shoes.

Price of shoes: $40
Producers make 100 pairs of shoes.

Consumers want 100 pairs of shoes at this price. Producers raise price to $30.

Consumers want 10 pairs of shoes at this price. Producers lower price to $30.

Consumers want to buy fewer shoes. Producers can afford to make more shoes.

Consumers want to buy more shoes. Producers cannot afford to make as many shoes.

Price of shoes: $30. Producers can afford to make 50 pairs. Consumers can afford to buy 50 pairs. Prices are at an equilibrium.

## Financial markets at work

As with markets for shoes, financial markets find a balance among the needs of different groups. Just as the shoe market makes the price of shoes consistent, the financial markets make the plans of savers and borrowers consistent with each other.

### Henry Ford and the Model A automobile

U.S. inventor Henry Ford (1863–1947) had a knack for taking things apart and putting them back together again. Growing up, he earned money fixing his neighbors' watches and almost anything mechanical he could get his hands on. He got a job as an engineer at the Edison Illuminating Company in 1891. But Ford wanted to produce automobiles. Most importantly, he wanted to make cars that offered better quality at a lower price than his competitors, so that everyone could afford to buy one.

Luckily, investors believed in Ford and his innovations, so they gave him the money he needed to turn his innovative ideas into goods that ordinary people could afford to buy. With this money, Ford was able to produce equipment that significantly improved the speed at which his automobiles were built—the moving conveyor belt, for example. Ford had a dream, and he succeeded. It brought him wealth and fame. But had it not been for investors and their willingness to bet on his ideas, Ford would have been like thousands of people throughout history who never had the chance to make their dreams come true.

Inventions like Henry Ford's affordable automobile would not have been possible without investors.

Unlike the shoe market, where prices are listed in dollars, the "price" that brings savers and borrowers together is the **interest rate**. This is the price that people pay over time for the chance to borrow money. It is also the amount that you earn if you "lend" the money to a bank by putting it in a savings account.

When interest rates are higher, people are more likely to put money in savings. This is because they will earn more interest on the money they invest. When interest rates are lower, people are more likely to borrow. This is because borrowing is less expensive when there is a low interest rate. The needs of different people eventually lead to an interest rate that keeps the financial markets moving forward.

## Investing for the future

When the needs of savers and borrowers are coordinated well, the market for borrowing money works smoothly. People and businesses with good ideas are able to get loans to build new businesses. They can also use investment money to find better ways to produce existing products and to create completely new products.

These investments may turn what seem like impossible dreams to one generation into conveniences the next generation takes for granted. Everything from cell phones to medicines to cars and airplanes are the result of inventors' ability to borrow in the financial markets (see box at left). We all benefit today from investments that have been made in education, research, machinery, and equipment.

## Risks and drawbacks

While such investments have great potential for improving people's lives, they are also risky. Many impossible dreams really are impossible. And even if they are eventually realized, it may be after years of failures and tremendous financial **losses** for those who invested in such high-potential, high-risk projects.

Even if investment is adding to the world's wealth and advancement, it does not always lead to happiness. New technologies may lead to workers being fired because they are no longer needed. For example, as automobile factories use more technology to make and assemble car parts, fewer factory workers are needed, and people lose their jobs. Yet at the same time, new technology can lead to new jobs that workers must be retrained for.

Investments are full of potential risks and rewards. The greater the risk, the higher the possible reward.

# Basic Investment Options

The financial markets offer a variety of investment options, depending on an investor's needs and goals. Each type of investment has its own risks and rewards.

The four major categories of financial instruments—which we will examine in the coming chapters—are bank deposits, **certificates of deposit (CDs)** or **time deposits**, bonds, and stocks.

## Bank deposits

Checking accounts, savings accounts, and **money market accounts** are all types of bank deposits. The key feature of bank deposits is that people can withdraw their money from the account at any time. Because of this ready access to money, compared to many other financial instruments, bank deposits have the lowest risk. In exchange for the low risk, people with deposit accounts can expect a lower **return**, meaning fewer earnings made from their investment.

Automated teller machines (ATMs) are a quick and easy way to access money you have in a checking or savings account.

## Checking accounts

People maintain checking accounts, also called demand deposits, in banks mainly for the convenience of paying bills with checks or debit cards. Most people do not open checking accounts with the goal of making money. You, as the depositor, receive little or no interest from the checking account. You may even have to pay a service fee if the balance (total amount) in the account does not reach a specified level and remain there. This is why many financial experts do not even consider a checking account an investment.

Putting money in a checking account is a loan to a bank. This is true of all the bank deposits discussed in this chapter. The bank can use your money to make its own loans.

## Savings accounts

Whether people are young or old, a common way to save money is by making a deposit in a savings account at a financial institution such as a bank, savings and loan association, or credit union. Compared to checking accounts, which have almost no risk but also offer no reward, savings accounts have a small amount of both.

Depositing money in a savings account is also a kind of loan to the bank. In return for your loan, the bank promises to pay a set interest rate on the money deposited. It then uses your money to make loans to borrowers who want to invest in small businesses or large companies, or to individuals who might want to use the money for large purchases such as a home or car. The bank charges more for the loans it gives out than it pays to depositors with savings accounts. In this way, banks make money.

With a savings account, the money is available to you whenever you want to take it out. Because banks offer this convenience, they pay a lower interest rate than with some other types of deposits.

### How do interest rates work?

Remember the laws of supply and demand in the example of the shoe market? (See pages 10 and 11.) The price for shoes was set by supply and demand. The same thing happens with borrowers and savers in the financial markets.

If too many people want to save or lend money at the going interest rate, and not enough people want to borrow it, the interest rate will go down. As a result, the demand for borrowing money increases. If the interest rate is so low that lots of people want to borrow money, but not many people want to save or lend, interest rates will tend to rise.

## Money market accounts

A money market account is another type of bank deposit that offers a slow but steady return at a low risk. Like a savings account, it is money that is deposited into the bank. However, there are more restrictions. You might be required to keep a certain amount of money in the account, or else be charged a fee if you take money out. And the money is not available whenever you need it. You might be allowed to withdraw from a money market account up to three times a month.

Thanks to these restrictions, banks have more freedom to invest the money deposited in these accounts—for example, to use it when they want to issue a loan. As a result, they offer a higher interest rate than they do for savings accounts.

## Certificates of deposit (CDs)

Another low-risk investment is a certificate of deposit, or CD. A CD usually pays a higher interest rate than money market or savings accounts. However, to get the higher interest rate, you have to agree not to withdraw your money for a certain period of time (called a **maturity** date). In some cases this is six to nine months, and in other cases it is up to five years.

As the owner of a CD, you earn a fixed interest rate over the specified time. If you withdraw money from the CD, you can lose some of that interest. Since you can only withdraw your money on a specified date without penalty, CDs are also known as time deposits.

CDs are very useful investments for at least two kinds of savers. The first kind are retired people who want to make sure that their money earns some return, but who also want to be sure there is no chance of losing their money. The second kind of savers are people who know they will need the money at a specific point in the future, which means they cannot take a chance on losing money. For example, a college student may have money saved for college tuition that will be due in six months. So, he or she would put the money in a six-month CD, where it will earn some interest but will also be perfectly safe.

With both bank deposits and time deposits, chances are slim that you will ever lose money. But with the investments discussed in the next chapter, you have a greater chance to earn a lot of money—but also the chance of losing it all.

## Weighing risk and return

The risk-return pyramid shown here illustrates the types of bank and time deposit accounts discussed in this chapter. The higher-risk investments higher up on the pyramid also offer the greatest rewards. With any investment plan, there is always a trade-off between risk and return on investment. This makes choosing the right investment more complicated. Should you just choose the financial instrument that gives the higher interest rate? Not necessarily. Those accounts that offer higher interest rates also have their own risks and drawbacks.

For instance, a time deposit (or CD) provides a greater return than a bank deposit, but it is also a greater risk for at least two reasons. First, the money in a CD is less available than the money in a bank deposit account. What if you faced a financial emergency? If you had to take the money out early, you would lose the interest you had earned on the deposit. You will get your money back, but not the interest you would have made.

Second, when you make a time deposit, you are paid a set interest rate until the maturity date. So if the interest rate increases after you open your CD, you lose the chance to invest the money in another account that offers a higher rate. Of course the interest rate could fall after you make your deposit, and because you are locked into the higher rate, you come out ahead. (For the top of this pyramid, see page 22.)

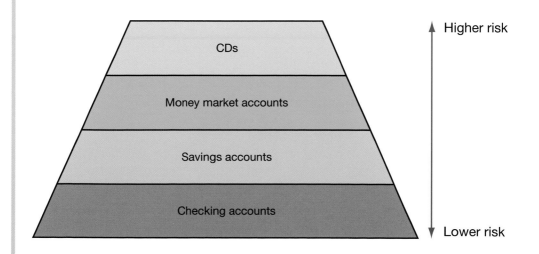

# Bonds

There are financial instruments that offer a better return on your investment than bank deposits and time deposits. Of course, the risk is higher, too. One such financial instrument is bonds.

## What is a bond?

When you buy a bond, you are loaning money to the organization that sold it to you—usually a corporation or a local, state, or national government. A bond pays a specified interest rate until a stated date of **maturity**. This means that you receive money from interest at regular intervals over the course of the year. Then, when the bond reaches its maturity date, you also receive back the full amount you originally loaned (the principal).

When you purchase a bond, you might receive a certificate like these. These certificates list details such as the bond amount and its maturity date.

For example, if you buy a $5,000 bond that pays 5 percent a year and matures in 10 years, you will receive $250 a year (5 percent of $5,000) for 10 years, and then at the 10-year mark your $5,000 will be returned. Or if you buy a $10,000 bond that pays 6 percent a year and matures in 10 years, you will receive $600 a year (6 percent of $10,000) for 10 years, and then your $10,000 will be returned at the 10-year mark. If you save and invest the $250 or $600 interest you receive in income every year, you would earn even more.

## Bond prices and interest rates

Most types of bonds have maturity dates that tell you when the principal will be repaid. However, a bondholder does not have to wait that long to get money back. Bonds can also be bought and sold on active bond markets (see box on page 20). The problem is that you may not be able to sell your bond for as much as you paid for it because of the changes in interest rates.

How does a changing interest rate affect the price of a bond? If interest rates increase after you buy a bond, then people will be able to find a bond that pays a higher rate than yours. As a result, your bond will no longer be worth as much if you want to resell it. On the other hand, if interest rates decline, the price of your bond will increase. People will pay more for the chance to earn the interest rate your bond earns.

## Interest rates and public debt

In recent years, many national and state governments have found themselves falling deeper into debt. For example, the United States owes more than $12 trillion in debt—or more than $60,000 per person. In the United Kingdom, the total national debt reached about 55 percent of what the country produces in a year.

In order to pay their expenses, these governments issue financial instruments such as bonds, which promise to pay the holder in the future, in exchange for their investment today. Government bonds are bought by individual investors, such as retirees, who wish to have very safe investments. These investors know that governments usually do not **default**, or fail to repay (see page 21). Government bonds are also bought by other countries. The Chinese government alone owns nearly $1 trillion worth of U.S. government bonds.

Selling government bonds helps fill the governments' immediate need for money. As governments fall deeper into debt, they try to sell more bonds and similar financial instruments. But if there are not enough people willing to invest in these instruments, interest rates will rise. As a result, governments will end up owing people even more interest on top of the countries' existing debt. The only way to reverse this situation is to start paying off government debt.

## Maturing bonds

The price you can get for a bond is affected by more than just changing interest rates. It is also affected by how soon the bond will mature. In general, the shorter the time until the maturity date, the less likely it is that the bond's price will change.

### How a bond works

Imagine that on September 1, 2009, you bought a three-year bond for $1,000 at an interest rate of 3 percent. You will receive an interest payment every six months. At the date of maturity, you will be paid back the amount of your investment. For your three-year bond, the maturity date is September 1, 2012. You will earn $15 every six months, or a total of $90, on your $1,000 investment. (See diagram below.)

What if you tried to sell the bond in April 2010? Whomever you sell it to will have a long wait until the investment is repaid, but will make $15 every six months along the way. If interest rates go up and the person could buy a bond with a higher interest rate, then he or she will not be willing to pay the full price ($1,000) for this bond. The person might only pay $980. But if interest rates go down, then your 3 percent rate will look pretty good, and the investor may be willing to pay more.

What if you sell your bond in March of 2012? Since there is only one interest payment left and the investment will soon be repaid, the interest rate does not matter much. You can probably sell it for close to $1,000.

| | $15 | $15 | $15 | $15 | $15 | Final interest payment plus principal is $1,015 |

Buy $1,000 bond on September 1, 2009  March 1, 2010  Sept. 1, 2010  March 1, 2011  Sept. 1, 2011  March 1, 2012  Maturity date: September 1, 2012

For example, if a bond with a face value of $10,000 matures tomorrow (meaning the owner will receive the final $10,000 payment tomorrow), its price will be very close to $10,000. The interest rate will not matter much because the bond will not earn much interest before it matures. For this reason, short-term bonds are usually less risky than long-term bonds. Because they are considered less risky, short-term bonds usually pay lower interest.

## Bond risks

While bonds are considered "safe" investments, they are not a sure thing. When you buy a bond, you are loaning money, usually to a business or a government. As with any loan, there is a risk that the interest promised will not be paid, or that the full amount of the money loaned will not be returned.

This risk is very small in the case of bonds issued by national governments with stable economies. The risk is a little greater with bonds issued by county, state, and local governments. The risk is somewhat greater still with major corporations with solid credit ratings, and even higher with bonds issued by corporations with serious financial problems, or new businesses with unknown prospects.

### Bond defaults

The risk of a government defaulting on its debts may seem slim, but it can happen. In 2001 the government of Argentina defaulted on the bonds it had issued to people around the world. Argentina owed bondholders about $95 billion USD (U.S. dollars), and its money reserves were almost gone. People saw the money they had invested for the future disappear.

Other governments tried to force Argentina to repay its debts. In the end, Argentina made a deal to trade the bonds that people held for new bonds that were worth only about one-third of the original value. Many bondholders were angry, but they had little choice, and most agreed to the deal.

This again shows the connection between risk and return. Government bonds typically pay low interest rates because they are the safest investment. The highest interest rates on bonds are paid on those issued by new companies with uncertain prospects. These companies' uncertain futures increase the risk that they will default on interest payments or on the repayment of the bond.

## Mutual funds

Investing in bonds does not always mean buying a single bond. Many people invest in **mutual funds** that contain many bonds. A mutual fund is a group of investments made by a financial services company on behalf of many investors. A mutual fund manager will choose a set of bonds that appear to be good investments. Investors can place money in the fund.

These funds have varying levels of risk and return. Some mutual funds contain only bonds, whereas others contain stocks, which are more risky. (See the next chapter for more on stocks.) Bond mutual funds provide a consistent return on your investment with less risk than investing in stocks. For this reason, bond mutual funds are popular among conservative investors who do not want high-risk investments.

## Pluses and minuses

Bond mutual funds carry an additional cost—the owner must pay a fee to the mutual fund company. Because they include many bonds, however, bond mutual funds also carry less risk. With a single bond, there is always a chance that the issuer of the bond will not be able to pay it back. With many bonds in a mutual fund, the risk is much less. This is a positive point about investing in mutual funds.

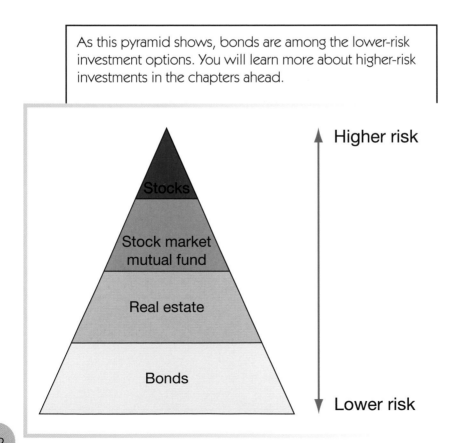

As this pyramid shows, bonds are among the lower-risk investment options. You will learn more about higher-risk investments in the chapters ahead.

Higher risk

Stocks

Stock market mutual fund

Real estate

Bonds

Lower risk

## Credit ratings and credit rating agencies

How can you tell if a bond is a safe bet or a risky bet? One way is to check the ratings given to the bond by a credit rating agency. These companies rate bonds on a scale of AAA to C. A rating of AAA on a bond indicates that the risk of default is very low. At the other end of the scale, a rating of C tells investors that the risk of default is very high. The organizations behind higher-risk bonds are likely to offer a higher interest rate, in order to attract investors who might otherwise be scared away.

Credit rating agencies have been criticized in recent years for their ratings. The purpose of credit rating agencies is to alert people when a financial instrument such as a bond is particularly risky. However, when risky new investments began to be offered in the late 2000s, rating agencies gave them high ratings, causing many people to lose money. Some people blamed credit rating agencies for the economic crisis that began in 2008 (see box below).

### Credit agencies in crisis

Did credit rating agencies cause the financial crisis and global **recession** (severe economic downturn) that began in 2008? Some people have argued that they played a large role.

In the late 2000s, investment companies began to offer new types of investments. They included groups of home loans that had been bought from banks and packaged together. Many of these loans were made to buyers who were at risk of defaulting on the loans (see pages 32 and 33). However, credit rating agencies gave these new investments high credit ratings. Since many people did not understand what was in these complicated new investments, they trusted the rating agencies and bought them, believing they were safe.

### Questioning the agencies

When people began to default on their loans and the investments people had made went bad, people began to look at the credit agencies more closely. Some people said that the agencies were too slow to lower ratings. Others said they had a close relationship with the companies offering the investments, so they were not giving an honest, objective report.

When it became clear that the investments were risky, credit agencies quickly lowered the ratings of many investments. This caused a panic that made many individuals and businesses afraid of investing at all. The unwillingness to lend or invest deepened the crisis. Many people came to believe that credit agencies need to change the way they rate investments.

# Stocks

The stock market allows people to easily buy and sell stocks. But what is a stock? A stock is a share of a business. For example, when you buy stock in Apple Computers, you become part-owner of that company. Depending on what you buy, you will probably only own a small share of the company. Hundreds or even thousands of other stockholders own the company alongside you. There are also institutional investors. These are organizations with huge supplies of cash (like banks and retirement funds). They invest this cash into company stock.

## Risks and rewards

When you buy stock in a company, you share in its risks and rewards. If business is good, the value of the company will rise, and your stock price will rise along with it. When things go wrong, stock prices will drop. And if the company goes out of business, your stock may be worthless.

As a part-owner of the business, however, you can have a say in how the company performs.

### Is the stockholder always right?

Some people have criticized the role stockholders play in business decisions. Stockholders often have only one goal in mind: making the value of their stock as high as possible. This means making the company as profitable as possible—sometimes at a cost.

For example, stockholders might be more willing to lay off workers if it makes the business more profitable. Or they might be willing to move a factory to a poorer country where labor is cheaper and environmental regulations are less strict. Of course, the same dangers are true of privately held companies. It is up to the business owners, whoever they are, to weigh how business decisions affect employees and the world around them.

Stockholders can attend meetings and make important business decisions. Businesses must work in the interests of the stockholders. Your voice is likely to be a small one, but it is a voice.

## The stock market

There is not one stock market, but rather many spread over the world. The New York Stock Exchange on Wall Street is the world's largest. Next is the Tokyo Stock Exchange, followed by the London Stock Exchange, which is the oldest stock exchange. Other stock exchanges exist around the world, from Ghana in Africa to Mumbai in India. The United States is home to two other major stock markets: the American Stock Exchange (for smaller companies) and the NASDAQ (for technology-based corporations).

## The trading floor

Most stock markets have a trading floor—a large room where people gather to make trades. The stock market trading floor is a hectic and noisy place. At the New York Stock Exchange, a bell rings to open and close trading for the day. Stocks are traded through a series of steps. Investors call stockbrokers to ask them to buy or sell a stock. Here is what happens when a broker receives an order to buy a stock:

1. The stockbroker calls his or her floor clerk, who is on the trading floor.

2. The trading clerk tells a floor trader about the order.

3. The floor trader finds another floor trader who is willing to buy or sell the stock. They agree on a price and the sale is made.

4. The final price is relayed back to the trading clerk, who passes on the information to the stockbroker, who alerts the buyer that the deal has been made.

## Electronic trades

Today, more and more stocks are being traded electronically. The NASDAQ is the world's first electronic stock market, and it has no trading floor. Everything is done remotely on computers.

The stock market floor is a noisy place where floor traders buy and sell stocks on behalf of investors.

## Investing in stocks

Investing in a corporation by buying its stock is generally considered a greater risk than buying a bond. As a part-owner, you get no promises on the return you can expect from holding the stock, or how much you will be able to sell it for in the future.

With luck, your stock will pay **dividends**. These are payments corporations sometimes offer to stockholders as a share of a company's **profits** (the total money made on top of costs). However, dividends are not always paid on corporate stock. More significant is the rise or fall of the value of the stock itself—which matters when you decide to sell your stock.

## Appreciation and depreciation

If the corporation is more profitable than expected, or if investors expect it to become more profitable, then the shares will **appreciate** in value (their price will increase). But if the corporation is less profitable than expected, or if investors expect it to be less profitable, then the shares will **depreciate** in value (their price will fall). If the corporation fails, the money from any assets sold—buildings, land, even furniture—will go to pay bondholders first, before any money is paid to the shareholders (owners of the corporation's stock).

If there is not enough to pay the bondholders the amount they have loaned the corporation, then the shareholders receive nothing, and their shares become worthless. Corporate stock shares are thus riskier than bonds, but they also can provide a greater return on an investment.

## Investing in individual stocks

There are several ways to invest in corporations by buying stocks. The first is to buy shares of stock of an individual corporation. This is risky, though. Because of the **volatility** (changeability) in the value of any given stock, the value of your investment will be highly uncertain.

The price of stock in a single corporation can drop significantly because of unexpected events. For example, the price of an airline stock can drop because its pilots go on a long strike or the price of fuel becomes very high. If a car company has to recall a vehicle because of a safety concern, its stock will drop. However, the price of an individual stock could also suddenly increase because of unexpected events. If a government changes the law to make it easier for a bank to earn big profits, for example, the stocks of banks are likely to rise.

Executives at Enron claimed to be confident in the company's future, even as its financial problems grew.

## The Enron scandal

One reminder of the danger of investing in a single company's stock came from the Enron scandal. This energy company was hailed as one of the most innovative companies in the world. It grew rapidly, and its stock reached as high as $90 per share. However, people in the company eventually realized that the profits were not real. The profits were the result of people knowingly misrepresenting the company's financial status. When the value of the stock peaked, executives began to sell their stock—knowing the true story of their finances, and that the stock's worth would soon dive as a result.

After executives sold their stock, the share price began to drop. However, executives encouraged people to buy or hold onto their Enron stock. Many employees had large amounts of money invested in Enron stock and trusted the company. They listened and held onto their stock. Eventually, problems within Enron were revealed, and the company collapsed. The stock prices dropped to zero, and many employees lost their retirement savings. Outside investors lost a lot of money, too. They learned all too well the dangers of investing in a single stock.

## Hedging your bets

How do investors avoid losing it all when the company they own stock in gets in trouble? They do so by investing in a variety of companies. If investors buy shares of stock in many different corporations in different industries, the risk of losing all of their savings is reduced.

Consider, for example, corporations that make umbrellas and corporations that make suntan lotion. Instead of buying nothing but stocks in an umbrella corporation, you could reduce the risk of your investments by buying some umbrella stocks and some stocks in a suntan lotion company. With nothing but umbrella stock, you are likely to see a drop in the value of your investment if it does not rain for a long time and the sun shines brightly. But if you also own suntan lotion stocks, the loss in the umbrella stocks will be moderated, and may be offset completely, by the rising value of suntan lotion stocks.

### High risk, high reward

Although buying an individual kind of stock puts you at risk of losing your money, there is also an opportunity for huge profits. In 1919, when the Coca-Cola Company began to sell shares of stock, an investor could buy one share for $40. If that investor bought that share and held it until December 1, 2004 (or passed it on to his or her grandchildren), the investment would be worth $191,544!

## Market ups and downs

Although investing in many stocks is safer than investing in a single kind of stock, sometimes this plan does not work, either. At times, the whole stock market seems to be going up or down.

Sometimes the market seems to be responding to the day's news. For example, a decision by a **central bank** to lower interest rates might lead to higher share prices, as people believe the new rates will boost the economy. (A central bank is a country's main bank, and it has power to regulate financial matters.) But news of a major military conflict might send share prices lower, as investors worry about business being disrupted.

Usually news only has an effect when it is unexpected. For example, say that people know the economy is doing badly and expect the unemployment rate to rise to 7 percent. Then the government announces that unemployment rose to 6.5 percent instead. This is bad news, but it is not as bad as people expected. As a result, stock prices may rise.

# Bull and bear markets

When there is a long period during which stocks as a whole are rising, it is called a bull market. And when there is a long period during which stocks are declining, it is called a bear market.

For example, the 1990s were a time of a bull market. When stocks began to fall in 2000, it marked the beginning of a bear market. Prices began rising again in 2003—another bull market—and dropped again in the bear market that began in 2008.

Sometimes it is difficult to tell which type of market you are in, as the market often rises one day only to fall the next. For example, look at the graph below. It tracks the Dow Jones Industrial Average, a collection of stocks that many people use to judge the stock market as a whole. Even though stocks were rising in late 2001, the bear market had not ended. But people did not know that until 2002, when stocks began to fall again. It is impossible to know for sure whether the market will rise or fall in the future.

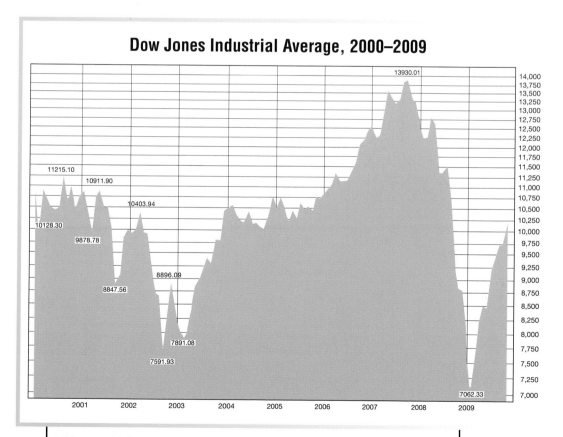

**Dow Jones Industrial Average, 2000–2009**

This graph shows the Dow Jones Industrial Average from 2000 through 2009. The stock market dropped dramatically several times throughout this decade.

## Stock mutual funds

As with bonds, stocks can also be bought through mutual funds. Mutual funds allow people to invest in the stocks of thousands of corporations with only a small amount of money. Some funds might contain only stocks, while others might include bonds, real estate, gold, and other types of investments.

Mutual funds became popular with ordinary investors in the late 1970s, and their popularity has been growing ever since. There are now thousands of different types of mutual funds offered throughout the world. Mutual funds generally offer a greater return than investors get from bank deposits, time deposits, or bonds, and they are not as risky as buying individual stocks.

### Managed funds

Most mutual funds are actively run by managers who decide which stocks to buy and sell. Mutual fund managers attract customers who believe the managers can "beat the market." This means they think the managers' wise investments will help them make more money than the stock market as a whole can offer at the time.

Some managers have made millions or even billions of dollars by making the right stock choices. For example, mutual fund manager Peter Lynch ran a famous fund known as the Magellan Fund for 13 years. He was able to pick stocks that rose in value by more than 29 percent each year—far better than the stock market average.

Does that mean that a good investor should go searching for a good fund manager? Not necessarily. On average, mutual fund managers do no better than the market as a whole.

Peter Lynch became a successful author and speaker after people learned of his skills as a mutual fund manager.

# Follow that stock!

It is easy (and can even be fun) to follow the progress of stocks. You can start by choosing corporations with publicly traded stock. Use an Internet site such as http://finance.yahoo.com or www.google.com/finance to track the stocks' performance for 10 business days. The chart below shows an example of the information you might find.

| Col. 1 52-WK HI LO | Col. 2 STOCK (SYM) | Col. 3 DIV & YLD | Col. 4 P/E | Col. 5 VOL | Col. 6 CLOSE | Col. 7 CHG |
|---|---|---|---|---|---|---|
| 39.04 24.81 | HRL | 0.76 (2.00%) | 16.81 | 475,966 | 38.37 | -0.27 (-0.70%) |
| 9.75 4.12 | XRX | 0.17 (2.15%) | 23.22 | 15,404,965 | 7.84 | +0.05 (+0.64%) |

**Column 1**: This reports the highest and lowest stock price during the most recent 52-week period.

**Column 2**: This shows the ticker symbol used for a stock. For example, the symbol used for shares of Hormel Foods Corporation's stock traded on the NYSE is HRL, and Xerox Corporation is XRX.

**Column 3**: This shows the dividends (DIV), or the annual payment per share to owners. If a dividend is paid, it is usually paid every three months (quarterly). It also shows the yield (YLD), which is the rate of return on a stockholder's investment. It is calculated by dividing the annual dividend by the current price of the stock.

**Column 4**: This shows the price-to-earnings ratio (P/E), which is determined by dividing a stock's price by the company's latest 12-month earnings per share. Some people believe a high price-to-earnings figure means that a stock is overvalued.

**Column 5**: This shows volume (VOL), which represents the total number of shares traded (in hundreds).

**Column 6**: This shows the last trade price for a stock at the end (the "close") of the previous trading day.

**Column 7**: This shows CHG, or change, which is the net change from the last trade price on the previous day and the last price on the preceding day. An up or down arrow may be used to represent whether the change was positive (+) or negative (-).

After you have followed the stocks for 10 days, ask yourself: Do these stocks seem to be rising or falling? Do they seem like a good investment? What might be affecting the value of these stocks? These are the sorts of questions people ask when choosing which stocks to invest in.

# Other Investments

The investments that have been discussed so far are some of the most common, but there are many more ways to invest money.

Some people invest in things that seem more "real" than a stock. They might buy a house or an apartment building in the hopes of reselling it in the future. Or they might buy precious metals or even works of art.

There are markets similar to stock and bond markets for some other investments. For example, people can invest in a fund that will rise if the price of an agricultural product such as grains or pigs rises. They can also invest in a foreign **currency** and hope that its value will rise compared to other currencies.

## Real estate

Real estate as a financial investment ranges from buying shopping malls and industrial factories to buying apartment buildings or houses. It is also possible to invest in real estate mutual funds. But the most common real estate investment occurs when people buy a home for themselves. Some people do not think of a house as an investment. Rather, they think of it as a place to live. But historically, buying a house has been a fairly safe investment. It slowly rises in value over time.

## The housing bubble

However, in recent years, people in many countries have invested too much in houses. Interest rates were low in countries such as the United States and United Kingdom in the 2000s, so it became easy to borrow money. Banks began to offer **mortgages** (loans to buy a home) that did not require putting a lot of money down. Two U.S. government–sponsored agencies made borrowing easier and made more money available for mortgages. They are called Fannie Mae (for the Federal National Mortgage Association) and Freddie Mac (for Federal Home Loan Mortgage Corporation). The extra money and lending made possible by Fannie and Freddie helped lots of low-income families buy homes, and this bigger demand added to the rise in home prices. But these people often bought homes they could not afford.

Home prices began to rise more quickly than usual, allowing people to buy a home, then resell it for a large profit. Many people believed that home prices could only go up. Soon millions of people were buying homes as money-making investments.

Home prices spiraled higher and higher, until they finally became too expensive to buy. Since housing prices had become too high for no good reason, people called the housing market a "bubble" that would soon "pop." People began falling behind on their mortgage payments. The people who had bought houses in the hopes of reselling them for a profit were unable to find buyers. Many people ended up with mortgages they could not afford, and millions of people lost their homes. (If a person cannot pay back a loan, the bank gains possession of the home.)

## Housing investment pluses and minuses

In a normal market, is buying a house a good investment? That depends on the individual. Earlier in life, you may find it better to rent, because young people tend to move more frequently as they change jobs or look for the perfect place to settle down. Buying a house also requires paying thousands of dollars at first—money that could perhaps be better invested somewhere else. And unlike other investments, it can be very difficult to sell a home quickly if you need the money.

### Lessons from the housing market

The rise and fall of the housing market in the 2000s holds many lessons. The first is that for most people, a house should be thought of as a place to live more so than as an investment. Second, doing what everyone else is doing is often not a good investment strategy. Many people bought homes because they wanted to make money by "flipping" them, or buying homes and reselling them for a profit. However, at that point there were many buyers in the market, pushing up the price. A better strategy might be to buy something that other people are not buying. In that case, the price may be low and have a better chance of rising over time.

For people planning to stay in one place for more than five years, a house can be a good investment. While rents increase, a homeowner usually has a set payment to make until the mortgage is paid. In many countries, owning a home also offers tax advantages. The interest you pay on your mortgage might not be taxed.

Some people buy houses and apartment buildings in order to rent them out. If the amount charged for rent is more than the mortgage payment, this can be a good investment. But investors also need to remember that being a landlord can be a lot of work!

## Trading currencies

Another form of investment is currency trading. Some people will invest in a foreign currency by trading the local currency for the foreign currency. If the foreign currency grows in value compared to the local currency, the investor will have made money.

For example, assume you own Euros and believe the British pound is about to increase in value compared to the Euro. You can use your Euros to buy British pounds at the existing exchange rate. Assume that 1 Euro can be converted into 1 British pound. This means that you can convert 100 Euros into 100 British pounds (not including the fees for buying and selling currencies). Assume that after using your 100 Euros to buy the 100 British pounds, the value of pounds does increase relative to Euros, with 100 pounds now worth 125 Euros. You have made 25 Euros minus your fees from your **speculation**, which is the risk you took with the hope of gain.

But speculation is risky and requires a lot of information and luck. The value of the British pound could have fallen relative to the Euro, and you would have lost money.

## Gold

Gold is a popular investment when people are worried that currency might lose some of its value. Since gold has been traded for thousands of years, people think of it as an investment that holds its value. But like any other investment, it can be a poor investment if it is too expensive at the time it is bought.

Investors can make money if the currency they have gains in value compared to other currencies.

## Speculating in commodities

Investors can also speculate on products called **commodities**—for example, agricultural products such as wheat and corn, as well as on other things such as cattle, pigs, metals, oil, coffee, and cocoa. They do this in commodity markets, sometimes referred to as futures markets. A commodity market for a certain type of wheat, for example, estimates the future price for the wheat. If an investor buys a contract to purchase the wheat at that price, and the price ends up being higher, then the investor can sell the contract for a profit. Prices for many of these commodities are greatly affected by weather, as weather affects the harvest. World demand also affects the prices of commodities.

One effect of a market like this is that it can increase today's price for a product. For example, in the late 2000s many people expected oil prices to keep rising. People traded for the chance to buy oil in the future, when they thought prices would be even higher. This belief actually had the effect of raising the price of oil. Believing that oil would be even more expensive tomorrow, people were willing to pay more for it today.

People can invest in agricultural products like pigs, too.

# Diversification and Compound Interest

Financial markets are the core of a productive economy. They bring together people who are saving with people who can use those savings to invest in the future. As a result, more money is earned and more products are created. The wealth in the economy increases.

Just as financial markets increase the wealth in the economy, they can also increase your wealth if you know how to use them.

## Understanding your goals

Saving and investing may reduce the amount of money you have available to spend in the short run, but it can greatly increase the amount you have to spend over your lifetime. How much you should save and how you should invest depends on your particular situation, objectives, and goals. Also, the financial instruments most appropriate for you depend on your purpose for saving and your tolerance for risk.

For example, money that will be needed for college in five years should be invested differently than money that will be needed for retirement in 50 years. Whatever your situation or objectives, though, you will be more successful in realizing your financial goals if you understand the importance of **diversification** and **compound interest**.

## A diversified portfolio

*Diversification* means reducing risk by holding a number of stocks from different corporations (remember umbrella and suntan lotion stocks?) or by holding several different financial instruments in your **portfolio**. (Your portfolio is your group of investments.) There is no way to completely eliminate the risk of losing money. But, through diversification, such risks can be lowered.

### Company stock

In past years, many employers have encouraged their employees to invest in company stock as a way of showing commitment to the company. However, this can be a very dangerous investment strategy. Investing heavily in any one stock is always risky (see page 27). In addition, if the company goes out of business, you may both lose your investment and be out of a job!

Many people try to reduce risk by investing in a mix of stocks, bonds, CDs, and other financial instruments. For people seeking to use their money soon, such as those who are close to retirement age, a financial portfolio may include lots of bonds and CDs, which are less likely to decrease in value. Those who will not use the money for many years are more likely to focus on stocks, which are riskier but usually make more money in the long run than other investments.

Diversified investment portfolios range from conservative to aggressive. The most aggressive investor might have all of his or her savings (or more) in stocks. At the opposite end of the spectrum is the most conservative investor, who might have all of his or her savings in bank deposit and time deposit accounts (CDs). Examples of what investment portfolios might contain for those who fall in between are illustrated in the charts shown to the right.

These pie charts show what investments might be made by a moderately conservative investor (top), a moderate investor (middle), and a moderately aggressive investor (bottom). Aggressive investors put more money into riskier stocks, which are likely to earn more money in the long term. Conservative investors will put more money into safer bets such as bonds.

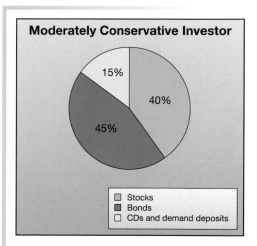

**Moderately Conservative Investor**

15%
40%
45%

☐ Stocks
■ Bonds
☐ CDs and demand deposits

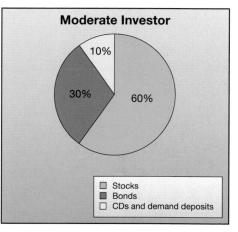

**Moderate Investor**

10%
30%
60%

☐ Stocks
■ Bonds
☐ CDs and demand deposits

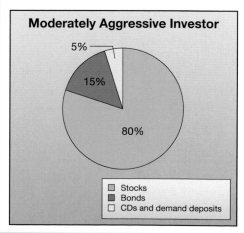

**Moderately Aggressive Investor**

5%
15%
80%

☐ Stocks
■ Bonds
☐ CDs and demand deposits

## Diversification and individual stocks

To reduce risk, an investor may diversify by buying 20 to 30 individual stocks in different industries for which changes in value tend to offset each other.

Think of the example of buying shares of stock in umbrella and suntan lotion corporations. Assume that an investment in umbrella stock goes up 40 percent a year when it is raining, and goes down 10 percent a year when the sun is shining. On the other hand, assume that suntan lotion stock goes up 40 percent a year when the sun is shining, and goes down 10 percent a year when it is raining.

Then let's assume that it rains half the year. If you have $100 to invest, you could invest it all in umbrella stock or all in suntan lotion stock, and your expected return would be the same in each case. On average, $100 in umbrella stock would earn $20 for half the year and lose $5 for half the year, for an expected $15, or 15 percent, return. This is the same return you will receive if you invest all of your $100 in suntan lotion stock. But if you invest everything in one industry, your return will tend to be unpredictable, with long periods of losses possible. It could be sunny for quite a long time, and if all your money is invested in umbrella stock, you could lose 10 percent a year. And the same is true if you invest all your money in suntan lotion stock, since it could be rainy for a long time.

### Diversifying

Now consider the result of diversifying your investments by putting $50 in umbrella stock and $50 in suntan lotion stock. In this case, you will get the expected return of 15 percent, no matter what the weather is. For example, if it is sunny for the entire year, you earn $20 from the suntan lotion stock and lose $5 from the umbrella stock—for a $15, or 15 percent, return. On the other hand, if it rains for the entire year you earn $20 on your umbrella stock and lose $5 dollars on your suntan lotion stock—for the same $15, or 15 percent, return.

## Stocks over the long term

While most investors are wise to invest in a variety of financial instruments, for those people who have a long time to wait for their investment to pay off, stocks can be the best investment. Over long periods of time, such as 20 years or more, stocks have typically produced better returns than bonds and other investments. Even so, wise investors do careful research before purchasing stocks, looking for the best long-term bets. Also, they do not overreact to short-term market fluctuations.

That advice can be hard to swallow during a long downturn. For example, look back at the graph on page 29, showing the rise and fall of the Dow Jones Industrial Average between 2000 and 2009. Investors who bought stocks in 2000 and kept it for 10 years would have found that their stocks most likely lost money.

However, looking at stock prices over a longer term gives a different picture. Look at this graph, which shows stock prices between 1900 and 2009. Over such a long period of time, the ups and downs of the 2000s look like a small blip on a steady rise. But sometimes the wait can be too long. Notice that after the stock market crashed beginning in 1929, it took more than 20 years for stock prices to recover.

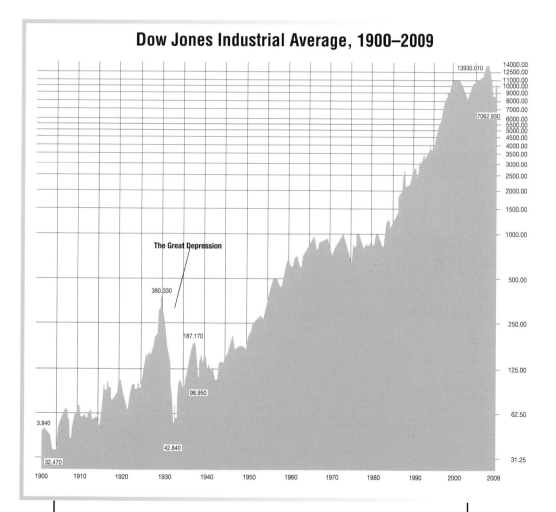

**Dow Jones Industrial Average, 1900–2009**

This graph shows the Dow Jones Industrial Average from 1900 through 2009. Although there have been many dips and falls, the market has always recovered and grown.

# Compound interest

Getting the largest return on an investment is clearly important. It may seem as though it takes a stock wiz to earn a lot of money, but the best strategy is sometimes simply to do nothing. If you invest your money early enough and let it sit and earn interest, your money can grow vastly through the power of compound interest, which is interest received by reinvesting the interest payments you receive.

The secret to benefiting from compound interest is to resist the temptation to spend the returns you earn from your investments. Spending the returns obviously makes sense for an older couple who plan to live off the interest payments of their savings, or off of dividends and appreciating investments, during retirement. But when you are young and want your savings and investments to grow, you may want to reinvest the money you make off of interest.

## Interest on top of interest

By not spending the interest earned on your savings this year, you can add the interest money to your total savings. You will then earn additional interest on this interest the following year. Do the same thing next year and you get interest on your interest on your interest, and so on. At first you will not notice this doing much to increase your wealth. But before long this compounding interest will begin to add up. And the more savings you have, the more interest you are earning to earn interest on, and the faster your savings grow.

Think of it as a small snowball rolling down a snow-covered mountain. Because it starts small, it does not pick up much additional snow (interest) and increases very slowly in size. But as it picks up more snow, it becomes larger and picks up more and more snow, which results in even larger amounts of snow being added to its size. Before long, it is a huge and rapidly growing snowball.

## Starting early

It is better to get a late start on a program of steady saving than never starting at all. But because of compound interest, starting early brings great benefits.

Compound interest will not add much to the amount you save right before retirement. But the money you saved years before retirement will have, through compound interest, accumulated and become a truly impressive amount of money by the time you retire. If you start the snowball near the bottom of the mountain, it will still be small when it stops rolling. It is the snowball that started rolling at the top of the mountain that is huge when it gets to the bottom.

## Every little bit counts

The power of compound interest can be illustrated with a simple example. Assume a young woman named Carol is considering eliminating the soda and pastry snack she buys every day. Instead, she will invest this money ($5 a day), starting on her 16th birthday.

If Carol decides against having this snack every afternoon, she will save $1,825 a year. Instead of spending this savings, Carol invests it in a mutual fund that provides an annual return of 6 percent a year in real terms—that is, after accounting for **inflation**. (Inflation is how it takes more money over time to buy the same amount of goods and services.) If Carol keeps this up for 10 years, she will have saved $18,250 by her 26th birthday. In addition to this, she will have accumulated $24,055 through compound interest. (We are assuming that she chose to have all of her return reinvested, to take advantage of compound interest.)

By skipping small purchases such as snacks and investing the money instead, an investor can build up a lot of money over time.

## Staying the course

The amount Carol has saved and the amount her savings are worth at each of several points over the rest of her life, beginning with age 26, are shown on this graph. As you can see, at age 26 Carol's payoff from compound interest has barely achieved liftoff. However, by continuing her saving plan, leaving all her return invested until she turns 36, Carol will have saved $36,508, but will have accumulated a total of $67,134. Continuing until her 46th birthday, Carol will have saved $56,575 and accumulated $144,281. The effect of compound interest has clearly accelerated. And now the benefits really start kicking in.

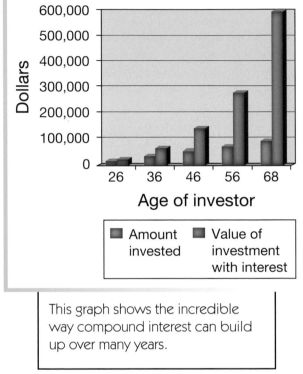

By the time Carol is 56 she will have accumulated $282,441 from saving contributions of only $73,000. And when she retires at age 68, she will have $599,114 from saving contributions of less than one-sixth that amount, or $94,900. Thus, by choosing not to eat and drink her snack every day and taking advantage of the power of compound interest, Carol has accumulated about $600,000 in retirement benefits!

This graph shows the incredible way compound interest can build up over many years.

## An expensive delay

The example of Carol can also be used to illustrate the importance of starting a saving program early. Assume that Carol had bought her daily $5 snack from ages 16 to 26, only then starting to save the price of a soda and pastry every day. It is good that she started her savings plan, and she will still benefit from the savings. But by postponing her saving program by 10 years, instead of having $599,114 on her 68th birthday, Carol would have $321,110. Delaying a 53-year saving program by 10 years reduces Carol's wealth at retirement by $278,004.

Many teachers rely on pensions as investments for their retirement.

## Pensions

Many people do not make their own decisions about how to invest. Instead, their employer offers them a **pension**. This is a fund that a company invests in on behalf of workers. When workers retire, they are entitled to income earned by the fund. Often the income is paid in fixed amounts.

Pensions can be safer than a personal investment plan because they offer a fixed income rather than an income that depends on the market. However, when people managing pension funds make risky investments, they can put the employees that depend on them at risk. Even though pensions are guaranteed amounts, some companies have reduced pension benefits for their employees when their investments did poorly.

Many companies have found that the money they owe employees is greater than the money that the pension plan is earning as an investment. As a result, some companies have stopped guaranteeing the amount of money an employee will make when he or she retires, instead making it dependent on the value of the fund.

# Market Volatility and Emotions

In the example of Carol's investment program on pages 41 to 42, we assumed the same return each year. However, because stock markets are volatile, investing in individual stocks will not always give you the same return. The ups and downs—the profits and losses—of the market can result in you having more or less money than Carol had after 52 years of investing. This is true even if you followed the same investment program she did and the market increased by the same amount.

Stock market trading floors are full of drama and excitement due to the volatility of the stock market.

## The effect of stock market increases

For example, if the market did not increase at all the first 50 years of your investment program, but increased so rapidly in the last two years that it caught up with the increase Carol experienced, then all the return would have occurred when you had a lot of money invested. In this case, you would end up with more than Carol.

On the other hand, if the market did all of its increasing over the first two years of your investment program, and then stayed the same for the next 50 years, all the return would have come when you had very little invested. In this case, you would end up with less than Carol. These are extreme examples, but they illustrate that the timing of stock market increases can affect the return you receive.

## Emotional ups and downs

The biggest problem with the ups and downs of the stock market is that it can cause investors to experience emotional ups and downs. These emotional swings often affect a person's investment decisions in a harmful way. Instead of staying with a steady investment program like Carol did, there is a strong tendency for people to buy and sell stocks in response to emotions—and this usually results in them getting a much smaller return than Carol received.

### Timing the market

Because no one can know what the stock market will do in the short run, the best strategy for most people when investing in stocks is to stay with a steady program of buying, like Carol. It is not wise to try to "time the market" by moving in and out. As we have seen, the stock market generally gives investors a higher return than other investments over the long term. Also, when you keep investing during stock market declines, you are benefiting from the opportunity to buy stocks even more cheaply than if the stock market were not falling.

## Fear of a downturn

When the stock market is dropping and people see the value of their investment getting smaller and smaller, it is natural for them to get worried. Markets can continue on a downward trend for a few years before starting to recover, with a full recovery sometimes taking even more years.

As the markets decline over time, worry can turn into panic, at which time a lot of people sell their stocks and put their money in safer (more predictable) financial instruments, like short-term bonds or savings accounts. But this is often about the time the stock market starts its recovery and starts paying higher returns than the safer investments.

## Fear of missing an upturn

Emotions can also motivate unfortunate investment decisions when the stock market is increasing. People who have sold their stocks at a large loss are understandably reluctant to repeat the experience, and so they tend to stay out of the market—and in their safe investments—as the stock market begins to head back up.

But if the stock market continues to rise, there will be news reports about all the money being made in stocks. These news reports will be supported (and often exaggerated) by comments from friends and associates about how well they are doing in the stock market. Before long, these reports can cause the fear of losing money in stocks to be gradually replaced by the fear of being left behind. The result is often that the people who sold stocks when stock prices were at or near their lowest point jump back into the stock market when prices are at or near a peak.

U.S. Federal Reserve Chairman Alan Greenspan worried that U.S. investors were suffering from "irrational exuberance." He felt that people were buying stocks based on emotion rather than common sense.

# "Irrational exuberance"

In the late 1990s, the rise of Internet-related stocks led to what many people later saw as emotional investment. The promise of the Internet led many people to believe that new Internet companies (also known as "dot-coms," after their web addresses) would be very profitable. Investors seemed to be offering money to anyone who had an idea for a new online business, and soon those businesses began offering stock. People raced to be the first ones to snatch up the stocks, sending share prices higher. However, many of these companies had little money or experience, and no real plan for making a profit.

As stock prices rose higher and higher, Alan Greenspan, chairman of the U.S. central bank, the Federal Reserve, commented that many investors were too optimistic and may be suffering from "irrational exuberance," meaning they were overly excited without really looking closely at the facts. He was proven right when stocks crashed in what was known as the bursting of the "dot-com bubble." Some companies saw their share prices tumble, while other companies disappeared entirely. Companies such as Pets.com spent millions on advertising, only to run out of money soon after. Lastminute.com in the United Kingdom saw its share price go from around 500 pence per share to 18 pence per share. It was soon clear that the mania over dot-com stocks was truly irrational.

## Investing during downturns

In 1929 John Raskob, an executive with General Motors (the U.S. automobile company), was interviewed for the magazine *Ladies' Home Journal*. In the interview, Raskob recommended a steady program of investing in stocks, predicting that this would return 24 percent a year over the next 20 years. The article containing Raskob's recommendation was published a few weeks before the start of the worst stock market decline in U.S. history, known as the Great Depression.

Over the next three years, the stocks on the New York Stock Exchange declined by 89 percent, as measured by the Dow Jones Industrial Average (see the graph on page 39). But despite the ridicule Raskob received for his comments in the article, his advice was actually good—even if his prediction was overly optimistic.

An investor who began investing just $15 each month (the amount Raskob suggested) in the stock market, beginning when Raskob's advice was published, would have done better after four years than the person who had invested the same amount in U.S. Treasury bills (the safest U.S. government bonds). In 20 years, the investor would have had $9,000 in wealth (far more than the Treasury bill investor), and in 30 years he or she would have had over $60,000 (having saved only $5,400 to buy stock).

This represents an annual return of 13 percent for 30 years. This is less than the 24 percent Raskob predicted, but still a return far greater than what would have been received by those who avoided the stock market crash by investing in low-risk bonds instead of stocks.

During the Great Depression, millions of people found themselves out of work and sometimes living on the streets.

## Young investors

When you are young, it is a good idea to start with an investment portfolio with many different kinds of stocks. This allows you to take advantage of the higher long-run returns from stocks.

Young people can even do well during bad periods for investors. For example, from 1929 until the early 1930s there was a sharp drop, or crash, in the stock market known as the Great Depression. Whereas the crash was a disaster for investors who were nearing retirement age, young people could have seen this as a tremendous opportunity rather than a loss. They would have had very little invested in the stock market, or anywhere else, when they were just starting their investment program. They could have bought stocks at very cheap prices and been able to hold onto the stocks for the long term, into retirement (see box at left).

## Taking advantage of financial markets

The old saying is true—money does make the world go around. Financial markets are critical to the functioning of the global economy. They keep the wheels of business turning. And if you invest wisely, they can improve your life by earning you money for the future.

Financial markets benefit you every day. They make it easier for suppliers to produce the goods consumers like you want now, to anticipate what you will want in the future, and to make the goods available at reasonable prices. These markets also provide you with opportunities to contribute to this productive process, by channeling your savings into their most valuable uses.

The best advice to earn money is both the simplest and the most difficult. It all comes down to saving rather than spending. The money you save and invest today is likely to grow greatly over time. By carefully saving and investing your money, you can take full advantage of the opportunities offered by the many forms of investment offered in the world today.

# Fact File

The following chart summarizes some of the main forms of investments covered in this book. Look back on the pages in parentheses to review each type of investment.

| DIFFERENT KINDS OF INVESTMENTS | |
| --- | --- |
| **Form of investment** | **What it does** |
| Checking account (page 14) | Keeps money conveniently available, but it may not earn any money |
| Savings account (page 15) | Money can be withdrawn when you need it, but it earns money slowly |
| Money market account (page 16) | Makes more than a savings account, but money is less available for use |
| Certificate of deposit (CD) (page 16) | Makes a set amount of money over time, but only if money is not taken out |
| Bond (page 18) | Earns a moderate amount of money, with a small risk of losing money |
| Stock (page 24) | Can earn or lose a lot of money |
| Real estate (houses and apartments) (page 32) | Usually rises in value (worth) over time, but is expensive and takes time to resell |
| Commodities such as gold, oil, or wheat (page 35) | Value can rise or fall due to world events that affect supply and demand |

# Risk-return pyramid

This pyramid shows the risks and rewards of various investments. Investments at the bottom have lower risk, but they also tend to offer lower rewards over the long term. Investments at the top have higher risk, but they also potentially offer greater rewards over the long term.

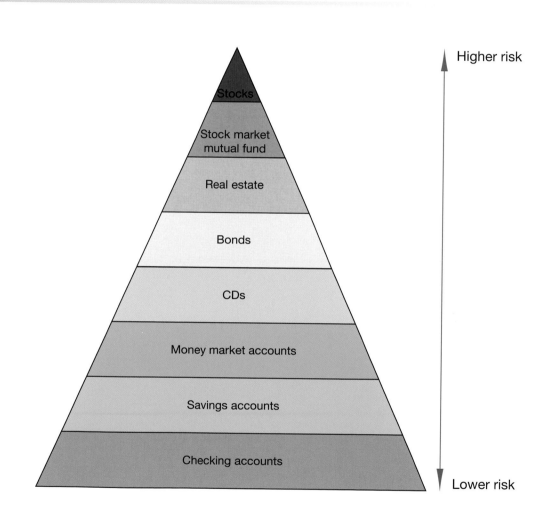

Higher risk

Stocks

Stock market mutual fund

Real estate

Bonds

CDs

Money market accounts

Savings accounts

Checking accounts

Lower risk

# Stock market returns

The graph below shows the rise in the stock market over more than 100 years, as measured by the Dow Jones Industrial Average. Although there were long periods of decline, such as from 1929 to 1931, overall the market has risen over time.

Although the stock market can rise over the very long term, it can also go through periods of extreme volatility, a fact reflected in the far-right section of this graph. As this shows, the stock market had moments of dipping dramatically throughout the 2000s.

## Dow Jones Industrial Average, 1900–2009

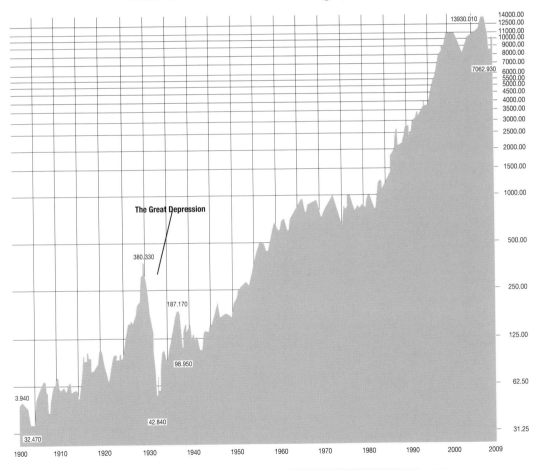

# Glossary

**appreciate** when the value or price of something, such as stocks, bonds, real estate, art, or diamonds, increases

**asset** item of value

**bond** investment that is a loan to the organization that sold it to you—usually a corporation or a local, state, or national government—that pays a specified interest rate until a stated date

**central bank** country's main bank, which has the power to regulate financial matters

**certificate of deposit (CD)** investment that earns a fixed interest rate over a specified time period; also called a time deposit

**commodity** product, such as oil, gold, or wheat, that can be traded

**compound interest** interest earned by reinvesting the interest payments received

**consumer** anyone who uses (consumes) a resource, good, or service

**credit** paying for an expense with borrowed money

**currency** money

**debt** money owed

**default** failure to repay

**demand** quantity of a good that consumers are willing and able to buy

**depreciate** when the value or price of something, such as stocks, bonds, real estate, art, or diamonds, decreases

**diversification** reducing risk by holding a number of stocks from different corporations

**dividend** part of a profit that corporations pay directly to shareholders (people who own stock in the company)

**economy** structures that shape the financial life of a country

**good** tangible item that provides value, such as an automobile

**income** earnings

**inflation** rise in the general price of goods and services

**interest** payment received in exchange for loaning money to someone; also, a payment owed in exchange for borrowing money from someone

**interest rate** amount of interest paid or received over the course of a year, as a percentage of the amount borrowed or loaned. For example, if you borrow $100 and pay $10 in interest at the end of the year, the interest rate is 10 percent.

**invest** lending money with the expectation of receiving benefits or rewards in the future

**investment**  money given with the expectation of receiving benefits or reward in the future

**investor**  anyone who lends money with the expectation of receiving benefits or rewards in the future

**loan**  money borrowed with repayment conditions

**loss**  used to describe when a person loses money on an investment

**market**  place where people buy and sell goods and services. It can be a specific location, like your corner grocery store, or it can be as extensive as the global market for oil.

**maturity**  date at which an investment is ready to be paid

**money market account** investment in which money is deposited into the bank, with some restrictions on when and how it can be accessed

**mortgage**  loan to buy a home

**mutual fund**  group of investments made by a financial services company on behalf of many investors

**pension**  fund that a company invests in on behalf of workers, to be paid when the workers retire

**portfolio**  individual's investments, including such things as the savings accounts, CDs, stocks, and bonds he or she owns

**price**  amount charged for a good or service

**producer**  person involved in creating goods and services

**profit**  money made minus the cost of expenses

**recession**  when an economy's growth slows down

**return**  earnings received from an investment

**risk**  chance that something will turn out differently than expected

**savings**  amount of money a person receives and puts away, rather than spending

**service**  performed action that has value, such as a haircut or having a car repaired

**speculation**  financial risk taken with the hope of gain

**stock**  share in a corporation

**supply**  quantity of a good or service that a business produces

**time deposit**  investment that earns a fixed interest rate over a specified time period; also called a certificate of deposit (CD)

**value**  benefit received from a good or service. Money is a common measure of value (as reflected in prices), although not all value can easily be measured in terms of money.

**volatility**  changeability

# Find Out More

## Books to read

Caldwell, Jean, et al. *Learning, Earning and Investing: Middle School*. New York: National Council on Economic Education, 2004.

Gilman, Laura Anne. *Economics* (*How Economics Works*). Minneapolis: Lerner, 2006.

Gwartney, James, Richard Stroup, and Dwight R. Lee. *Common Sense Economics: What Everyone Should Know About Wealth and Prosperity*. New York: St. Martin's, 2005.

Leet, Don R., et al. *Institutions and Markets* (*Focus*). New York: National Council on Economic Education, 2003.

## Websites

"Biz Kids"
**www.bizkids.com**
This website offers lessons to help young adults become financially educated, learn work-readiness skills, and find out how to become entrepreneurs.

"A Write to Learn: Money Lessons"
**www.awritetolearn.com/money_lessons.htm**
What do exchange rates have to do with the Olympics? How can you budget your money and reach your money goals? Find out at this website.

"Council for Economic Education"
**www.councilforeconed.org**
This organization provides training and materials to educate teachers and students throughout the world on economics and finances.

"It All Adds Up: Personal Finance for Teens"
**www.italladdsup.org**
Play games and learn how to budget, buy a car, pay for college, save, invest, and use credit cards at this website.

# Index